Voice of the Grasslands

Whispers in the emerald sea,
Where silent winds weave tapestry.
Morning dew on blades of green,
Hints of life in every sheen.

Gentle whispers of the breeze,
Talk to flowers, sway the trees.
Nature's choir, wild yet free,
Sings the song of destiny.

Beneath the sky, so vast, so grand,
Lives the voice of the grassland.
Silent power in its flow,
In its care, all life does grow.

Golden Roar

At dawn's first light, it sings to the sky,
The golden roar where the eagles fly.
Mountains echo, valleys ring,
With the power each note can bring.

Sunrise painted, horizons dared,
Nature's orchestra well-prepared.
Symphony of the light reborn,
In the heart of the golden morn.

Cascading rays on earth do surge,
Melding night with day—a gentle urge.
In the warmth of morning's lore,
Rises strong, the golden roar.

Eternal Dominance

Stars blink in the velvet night,
Witness to an unrivaled might.
Planets spin in silent trance,
Under skies of eternal dance.

Galaxies in endless sprawl,
Silent titans in a cosmic hall.
Power etched in every glance,
Marking fate with eternal dominance.

Time itself bends to this reign,
A ruler of infinity's domain.
In the vast, eternal night,
Dominance rules with might and right.

Noble Roar

In the heart of ancient tales,
Mountains stand, and rivers veil.
Fierce and silent, yet so pure,
Nature boasts its noble roar.

Battles fought and legends born,
In the cradle of the morn.
Majesty in every core,
Resounds with strength, the noble roar.

Valleys listen, peaks proclaim,
An echo carrying endless fame.
In every brook, in every shore,
Lives forever the noble roar.

Magnate of the Wild

In the heart of grasslands vast,
Where shadows stretch and play,
The magnate of the wild stands fast,
In golden hues of day.

With every mighty roar that's sung,
He claims the land as his,
Beneath the sky where stars are hung,
In twilight's gentle kiss.

His paws have tread where few have gone,
Through rivers wide and deep,
The dawn's first light, a promise drawn,
In secrets he will keep.

Whisper of the Pride

The whisper of the pride we hear,
In evenings soft and still,
A language known to hearts so near,
It carries through the hills.

In unity, they share their tale,
Of trials and triumphs grand,
Through storm and sun, in moon's soft veil,
Together they will stand.

Each gesture, glance, and fleeting touch,
With grace they interlace,
A symphony that means so much,
A family, embraced.

Mane's Command

With mane aglow in twilight's gleam,
He strides with regal air,
The jungle bows, a living dream,
To power laid bare.

His eyes survey the kingdom wide,
In silence they obey,
With every step, his chosen stride,
The night becomes his day.

He rules with wisdom deep as night,
With courage firm and true,
And in his gaze, the stars ignite,
The world is born anew.

Courage of the King

In shadows deep where dangers creep,
He stands without a fear,
The courage of the king will keep
The wild ones drawing near.

His heart, a beacon through the gloom,
A light in darkest times,
Dispelling every whispered doom,
With strength that soars and climbs.

His roar, a herald of the dawn,
His pride within his chest,
In battles fought and victories won,
He stands above the rest.

Feline Throne

In shadows deep, the cat does reign,
Its silent rule, a soft refrain,
Eyes gleam bright in moonlit night,
A sovereign pure in silver light.

Paws tread light on regal ground,
A kingdom quiet, without sound.
Whiskers quiver, senses keen,
The feline monarch, rarely seen.

With every leap, the power shows,
Graceful arcs the dark bestows.
Silent watcher, mystic gaze,
In night's embrace, its spirit stays.

From lofty perch, it spies the land,
Each subject waits for silent command.
Mighty hunter, subtle knight,
In dreams, it rules the velvet night.

The throne is shadow, yet profound,
In every heart, its home is found,
The feline sits, its empire vast,
In realms of midnight, first and last.

Golden Dominion

Sunrise cracks the twilight sky,
With promises of bright new highs,
Light pours forth, a gilded stream,
Unveiling dreams once held in gleam.

Fields awash in morning's gold,
A kingdom new, stories unfold.
Nature's crown, in rays adorned,
Golden dominion newly born.

Mountains bathed in amber hue,
As morning's light makes day anew.
In every leaf, a spark is found,
Boundless beauty knows no bound.

Rivers glisten, pure and bright,
Mirroring the dawn's soft light,
Golden riches, vast and free,
Embrace the world in majesty.

Empire of warmth, the sun bestows,
Where every heart with fervor glows.
Golden dominion, fierce and fair,
Nature's splendor, beyond compare.

Ruler Among Beasts

In jungles vast, a lion's roar,
Proclaims the king forevermore.
Golden mane, with regal grace,
Commands respect through time and space.

Paws that thunder, might unbound,
Sings a song of primal sound.
In verdant realms, it reigns supreme,
A ruler born from ancient dream.

Eyes that pierce the deepest night,
Guardians of the wild with might.
Every creature hears its call,
In the lion's reign, they stand in thrall.

Savannah's prince, in daylight's blaze,
Majestic strides, a proud display.
Nature's power, raw and pure,
Within the lion, strong and sure.

In every roar, the world takes pause,
A ruler just, with iron claws.
Royal beast, both fierce and grand,
In wild domain, it holds the land.

Harbinger of Dawn

Night's retreat, as shadows fade,
Reveal the dawn, in light parade.
Harbinger of day's embrace,
Awakens world in softest grace.

Stars give way to morning's breath,
A silent pledge that conquers death.
Sky ignites in crimson hues,
A touch of gold in twilight's shoes.

Birdsong heralds the breaking light,
With melodies that conquer night.
Every note, a promise sweet,
Of warmth and hope in dawn's heartbeat.

Mountains greet the coming sun,
Another day has just begun.
Harbinger of new-found dreams,
Infuses life with brilliant beams.

In every dawn, a tale unfolds,
Of endless light, and courage bold.
Harbinger of dawn, so bright,
Guides us gently from the night.

Lord of the Hunt

In shadows deep, where moonlight bends,
The hunter's call, the forest sends.
With silent steps, through twilight's haze,
He claims his prize, in ancient ways.

A bowstring taut with whispered strength,
Through tangled paths, at arm's length.
His keen gaze sharp, the night is his,
The primal dance, his soul to quiz.

The forest stirs with secret sound,
A sacred bond, forever bound.
The hunt, the chase, the evening sky,
In nature's arms, the spirits fly.

Wolves may howl and owls may cry,
But he moves like wind, swift and sly.
A glimpse of him, the heart will pound,
For he is king, where wild things are found.

Tusker's Foe

Through jungle dense, where giants roam,
A shadow creeps, far from home.
With spear in hand and eyes like steel,
He faces beasts, whose power is real.

The tusker's roar, the earth does shake,
But he stands firm, for courage's sake.
He knows the path through danger's tread,
A warrior's way, where angels dread.

Each step calculated, breath is measured,
In dim lit glades, his life is treasured.
A dance of death, in twilight gleamed,
Where battles fought, and victories dreamed.

With heart that beats like tribal drum,
He vows to never turn and run.
For he's the hero, legend's seed,
Against the tusker, in word and deed.

Voice of Authority

From marble halls and gilded throne,
A voice declared, in steadfast tone.
With clarity, the words did rise,
The truth unveiled, no room for lies.

Commanding hearts and bending will,
With justice served, he stands so still.
In every law, his echo sound,
The people trust, in him they're bound.

His eyes see far, beyond the veil,
Through winds of doubt, like ship through sail.
The hand that guides, the words that bind,
In him they find, a savior kind.

Kings may fall and crowns may fade,
But his decree, in stone is laid.
For he's the voice that tempests quell,
Authority's shield, where freedom dwell.

Regent of the Wild

In verdant realms, where rivers flow,
The wild regent claims his throne.
Amongst the trees, his court convenes,
With creatures grand and verdant scenes.

His crown of leaves, his robe of moss,
He reigns without a sense of loss.
In harmony, he rules the land,
With nature's law beneath his hand.

The whispering winds, the chorus sings,
Of forest tales and ancient kings.
His scepter, wood, his grace untamed,
In wild embrace, he's rightly named.

No walls confine his boundless state,
The stars his guide, the moon his mate.
With every breath, the world does smile,
For he's the regent of the wild.

Realm Reap

In fields where shadows gently creep,
The harvest whispers secrets deep,
Of ancient lands where echoes sleep,
The realm we call, the dream we keep.

Golden waves dance in the breeze,
A symphony among the trees,
Whispered tales of distant seas,
In realms untouched by time's decrees.

Stars above like guardians gleam,
Casting light upon the stream,
Where wishes float, and hopes redeem,
In the gentle realm of dream.

Silent night on velvet spread,
Dreams converge where stars have led,
In this harvest, paths are tread,
Between the worlds of living and dead.

A realm that's hidden, out of sight,
Reaped in shadows, day and night,
Where dreams and whispers reunite,
In the softest glow of twilight.

Royal Allocation

In halls of gold and tapestries,
The tale of kings and bound decrees,
Of royal blood and legacies,
The crown bestows without appease.

A throne of power, ancient, wise,
Sees through time with sovereign eyes,
Allocating fate's disguise,
Amongst the stars and lunar skies.

Pages turn in history's book,
Where future kings and queens will look,
Destiny's course, by fate's own hook,
In royal hands their lives they took.

Beneath the robe and jeweled clasp,
Responsibilities they grasp,
An era's weight within their clasp,
Determined by the royal asp.

Upon this path, they shall not veer,
In duty's call, they persevere,
With wisdom guiding, crystal clear,
The royal allocation here.

Leader's Lot

Upon the path where shadows fall,
A leader's cry, a clarion call,
With courage, strength, they stand up tall,
To forge the future, one for all.

Through trials faced and battles fought,
Wisdom earned and lessons taught,
A leader's way is seldom sought,
Yet in their heart, the dream is caught.

In darkest night, when hope is dim,
Their beacon light will never trim,
Steadfast they stand, unyielding limb,
With every challenge, no mere whim.

They bear the weight, with honor crowned,
In service true, where truth is found,
Their oath to lead, a sacred bound,
To lift the weary from the ground.

For in their soul, a fire burns,
A guiding star, the world discerns,
A leader's lot, the path it turns,
Toward the light, as dawn returns.

Dominant Slice

In circles grand where power plays,
The dominant slice of fleeting days,
With influences that time outweighs,
Their footprints carve through the haze.

An empire's rise, a kingdom's fall,
Where history echoes in this hall,
The dominant stand, commanding all,
With visions vast and voices tall.

They shape the path of future's gaze,
Through winding turns and labyrinth's maze,
Their will a force that binds and stays,
In every act, their soul they raise.

Beneath the sun and moon's embrace,
They forge ahead at steady pace,
In power's dance, they find their place,
A slice of life, a steady grace.

This dominant slice of fate's own pie,
With wings to dream and hopes to fly,
They grasp the reins, with eyes on sky,
To lead, to conquer, and to try.

Plains' Protector

Under skies of endless blue,
The windswept plains extend,
A guardian stands in view,
Nature's stalwart friend.

With gaze both fierce and bright,
He surveys the land,
Through day and through night,
A watchful guiding hand.

Grass bends in whisper's touch,
Beneath his steady stride,
He knows each curve and crutch,
Of where the wild things hide.

Unyielding as the stone,
Yet tender as a breeze,
In his heart alone,
The secrets of the trees.

When twilight cloaks the day,
And stars begin their play,
Guarded, safe, you'll stay,
In his watchful sway.

Crowned Grasper

On lofty peaks, he reigns,
With talons sharp as swords,
The monarch who maintains,
Dominion over fjords.

His wings in mighty span,
Cast shadows wide and deep,
An ever-watchful plan,
No secrets shall he keep.

His eyes, like burning gold,
Survey the realms below,
Through tempests crisp and cold,
In sun, in rain, and snow.

A crown of feathers grand,
Worn with regal grace,
He grasps the fortress land,
In a fervent embrace.

Where mountains kiss the sky,
His cry, both bold and free,
Resounds from high to high,
A king in majesty.

Aura of Authority

In halls of ancient lore,
Where shadows weave their tales,
An aura flows from yore,
Through time's unyielding gales.

A presence vast and grand,
Commands the space it fills,
With unseen, gentle hand,
It bends both hearts and wills.

A whisper soft yet strong,
Echoes through the night,
In dreams where all belong,
To realms of purest light.

Ascended from the past,
To bless the present day,
Its light and shadows cast,
Guide souls along their way.

In stillness, it resides,
An ever-glowing star,
Through life's eternal tides,
An anchor from afar.

Dominant Roarer

Upon the savannah's swells,
Where golden grasses sway,
A mighty presence dwells,
To mark both night and day.

His roar beneath the sun,
Commands the boundless plain,
In battles lost or won,
His strength shall still remain.

With mane of burnished gold,
And eyes that gleam like fire,
His legacy unfolds,
Through courage and desire.

The shadows of his form,
Cast far across the land,
In peace or in storm,
His power does expand.

As twilight gently falls,
And stars adorn the skies,
His voice, both fierce, enthralls,
The ruler never dies.

Roar of Power

In shadows deep, the lion waits,
With golden eyes and heavy gait,
The dawn breaks clear, the air abate,
His roar of power resonates.

Across the plains, his call will soar,
A beacon strong, a primal lore,
In every heart, a fear restores,
Nature's king on earth and more.

With every stride, he claims his land,
A silent rule, an unseen hand,
The savannah obeys his command,
In his kingdom, alone he'll stand.

The sun dips low, the night descends,
His legacy, the wind suspends,
A tale of power, time transcends,
In the lion's wake, no pretends.

In every beat, his heart's refrain,
A rhythm pure, a wild domain,
The lion's roar, a timeless strain,
Echoes eternal in reign.

Safari's Apex

Beneath the blazing African sky,
Where zebras graze, and eagles fly,
The lion strides, no hint of shy,
A monarch's gaze, a watchful eye.

He reigns supreme, in golden mane,
Across the veldt, through sun and rain,
Without a crown, without a chain,
His rightful place, he will maintain.

The herd seeks shelter, awed by might,
As dusk turns into quiet night,
In shadows deep, he'll claim his sight,
A predator, in silent flight.

With every breath, his strength displays,
A creature born of ancient days,
In regal poise, he softly lays,
The apex of the safari's ways.

And as the stars spread far and wide,
The lion's pride will never hide,
A testament to nature's stride,
In him, all silences confide.

Safari Sovereign

In the heart of the endless plain,
Where wild whispers can't be tamed,
The lion rules, majestic claim,
A sovereign's peace, a sacred name.

Beneath acacias, among the rills,
His presence, felt in all the chills,
A silent grace, the air it fills,
In every gaze, the world he stills.

His kingdom vast, with no confines,
Each rival learned, each foe declines,
In his domain, the sun defines,
A wilderness, where power aligns.

From rocky cliffs to river's edge,
Through golden fields and eden's hedge,
The lion roams with timeless pledge,
A sovereign strong, with every fledge.

As dawn begins its gentle rise,
Reflects the truth in lion's eyes,
A world untouched by man's disguise,
In nature's realm, the sovereign lies.

King of Wilderness

Through grasses tall, he strides alone,
A king without a somber throne,
His realm, the wild, the great unknown,
A legacy in nature's tone.

With every step, the earth reveals,
A kingdom vast, the heart it heals,
In shadows deep, his strength conceals,
A predator, truth in appeals.

The gazelles leap, the insects hum,
To his silent court, they become,
A lion's gaze makes senses numb,
In wilderness, no rule to succumb.

The dusk draws near, the stars ignite,
In moonlit beams, his figure bright,
The night's refrain, a lion's rite,
In darkness, power's purest light.

He reigns across the endless miles,
Through desert's breath and forest aisles,
His legacy in nature's files,
The king of wilderness, no trials.

Apex Possession

Upon the summit, hearts conspire,
Beyond the reach of man's desire.
Infinite dreams, the heights reveal,
Eternal echoes, their appeal.

Where stars converge in cosmic dance,
And fate unveils, given chance.
Specters of light, in twilight's grip,
Guiding souls on heaven's ship.

Peak of marvels, mystic embrace,
A boundless realm, no time to trace.
Eyes cast upwards, lost in flight,
In moonlit whispers of the night.

First Feast

Beneath the harvest moon's soft glow,
A table set in autumn's flow.
Nature's bounty, rich and grand,
Shared with love, hand in hand.

Whispers of leaves in twilight's breeze,
Stories told 'neath ancient trees.
Golden fields, the sun's embrace,
Unity in every face.

Fire's warmth, a glowing hearth,
Echoes of laughter, joy's rebirth.
Bonds anew, with every bite,
First feast shared in evening's light.

King's Keep

In stone halls, where legends grow,
A king's command, with regal glow.
Armored knights in shadow's sweep,
Guard the secrets, a world asleep.

Tales of valor, etched in gold,
Whispers of battles, brave and bold.
Flames of torches, fierce and bright,
Echoes of honor, in the night.

Banners waving, high and proud,
Voices rising, clear and loud.
In the keep, where dreams are sown,
A monarch reigns, his fate unknown.

Jungle's Justice

In verdant depths, where shadows play,
Predators roam, night and day.
Rustling leaves, a hidden court,
Justice served, in wild's retort.

Nature's law, both fierce and fair,
In jungle's grip, all must beware.
Every howl, the night's decree,
Balance kept, eternally.

Untamed spirits, bound in oath,
To the silent, verdant growth.
Cycle of life, relentless sweep,
Jungle's justice, buried deep.

Imperial Income

In halls where whispers ebb and flow,
The coins of ages softly glow,
Each shimmer speaks of old disguise,
A kingdom built on traded lies.

Gold threads that weave through time and space,
Binding fortunes in their place,
From crown to pauper, all the same,
In endless chase of wealth and fame.

Riches gathered, fleeting strains,
In cycles of abundance, pains,
What price the coffers, filled with care?
The weight of gold, a common snare.

Through tunnels dark and vaults concealed,
The secrets of the wealth revealed,
From crumbling tombs to royal halls,
All succumb to fortune's calls.

Thus flows the imperial stream,
A river wrought of gilded dream,
In shadows cast by ancient might,
The treasure gleams in humble light.

Throne's Treasure

Upon the throne, where power lies,
A wealth unseen by common eyes,
Beneath the seat, a vault of dreams,
Where ambition flows like silver streams.

Echoes of triumph, battles won,
Stored within, beneath the sun,
Jewels and relics, tales untold,
In silence keeps the secrets bold.

Emeralds glisten, rubies blaze,
Reflecting light in royal gaze,
Each gem a story, each crown a mark,
On history's vast and mighty arc.

Yet treasures hold a heavy weight,
For those who guard and seal their fate,
In chambers deep, where shadows dance,
The price of riches is a chance.

So guards the throne its hidden prize,
Behind the mask of regal guise,
For in the end, what lies therein,
But echoes of a kingdom's sin?

Supreme Spoils

In battles fought and wars long past,
The spoils of victory hold fast,
From empires built on marshal might,
The prizes gleaned in darkest night.

Gold and silver, bright and keen,
Pillage taken, lands serene,
Weapons forged in fires bright,
Symbols of a sovereign's right.

Through the ages, wars repeat,
For lands, for power, riches sweet,
The cycle turns, the spoils gleam,
In every victor's wildest dream.

But victory's spoils, so dearly earned,
Are tales of those who've never returned,
And in their shadows, glory fades,
Replaced by hollow, fleeting shades.

So claims the warrior his due,
In lands of green or skies of blue,
Yet supreme are the spoils to see,
For fleeting, fragile, they must be.

Jungle Juxtaposition

In verdant depths where secrets lie,
The jungle hides its knowing eye,
A world of contrast, day and night,
In shadows deep and dappled light.

Beneath the canopy so vast,
The whispers of the ages past,
A dance of life, of tooth and claw,
The jungle holds its silent law.

Bright blooms that flaunt their vivid hues,
Against the leaves of varied cues,
A riot of creation's hand,
In chaos ordered, mystic land.

Yet there within the jungle's heart,
The cycles play their hidden part,
Birth and death, a balancing,
In nature's grand and boundless ring.

In jungle's world, the seen, unseen,
By senses sharp or senses keen,
A juxtaposition wild, untamed,
Where life and death remain unclaimed.

Symbol of Might

In golden fields, the lion roams,
With regal stance, his power known.
Beneath the sun, his mane does blaze,
A symbol of strength, in nature's daze.

Eyes of amber, sharp and keen,
Surveying lands where he's the king.
Through jungles dense and plains so wide,
His roar echoes, none can hide.

Majesty strides with each paw print,
Marking territory with every stint.
The crown he wears, though made of fur,
Proclaims a legacy, timeless and pure.

In midnight hours, or dawn's first light,
His shadow moves, a fearsome sight.
Guardians guard, yet tremble still,
At the lion's will and unmatched skill.

Noble heart, defying foes,
The might of the lion forever grows.
In silent woods or bustling lands,
His legend lives, unyielding, grand.

Ferocious Reign

Through savannahs, wild and free,
The lion reigns with authority.
Ferocity in every stride,
In his kingdom, power resides.

His roar commands the endless skies,
As echoes dance, the world complies.
Under his gaze, all creatures cower,
Acknowledging his daunting power.

Untamed spirit, fierce and bold,
A legacy of ancient stories told.
In battles fierce, his strength prevails,
Marking victory with each tale.

Majestic mane in moonlight shines,
A symbol of primordial lines.
His empire vast, from east to west,
In his presence, all creatures rest.

Through ages past and days ahead,
The lion's reign, in power spread.
His name, a whisper on the wind,
A tale of might that will not rescind.

Majesty Among Beasts

In the heart of the jungle, deep and wild,
The lion walks, untamed and unbeguiled.
With grace and power, he claims his throne,
A king revered, forever known.

Upon the hill, he stands so tall,
His presence rules over all.
Nature bows, and whispers sing,
Of the majesty that he does bring.

Mane of gold, and eyes that gleam,
In sunlight's glow or moon's soft beam.
He strides with purpose, confidence clear,
A leader among beasts, none come near.

His realm extends from den to shore,
Across the land, his roar does soar.
A signal of his sovereign might,
Echoing through the darkest night.

In tales of old and dreams anew,
The lion's pride remains true.
Majesty lives in every breath,
A symbol of strength, enduring death.

Lionhearted Rule

With courage born beneath the stars,
The lion stands, with battle scars.
Heart of steel and spirit pure,
His rule is just, his kingdom sure.

Beneath the sky, both day and night,
He guards his realm, in endless fight.
With every roar, a promise made,
To protect his land, come what may.

Majesty flows in every vein,
A lion's pride, through joy and pain.
In fields of gold and forests green,
His presence felt, his power seen.

Through trials faced and battles fought,
His lionhearted rule is sought.
With wisdom deep and courage true,
A reign of strength both old and new.

Legends tell of his great might,
Of a lion's heart that shines so bright.
In stories carved on ancient stone,
Forever will his rule be known.

Apex in Amber

In lands where sunsets brush the sky,
The shadows of the dusk draw nigh.
A golden gaze, a hunter's stare,
With strength and courage, beyond compare.

An emperor of grass and sand,
Ruling with a subtle hand.
A kingdom vast, a silken throne,
In amber light, his prowess shown.

The whispers of the twilight wind,
Echo tales of where he's been.
Through realms untamed, through nights profound,
Where silent paws make not a sound.

In twilight's glow, the hunt unfolds,
With stories that the night beholds.
Amber eyes that pierce the night,
A lion's heart, a warrior's might.

Across the plains, the proud one roams,
In amber sea, he makes his home.
Majestic, fierce, forever free,
Apex in amber, eternally.

Highness of Claws

In the realm where the wild things sleep,
A sovereign roams, through jungles deep.
Claws as sharp as morning's glint,
Moves with stealth, leaves not a hint.

On lofty peaks, beneath the moon,
He sings a silent, distant tune.
A creature formed by nature's laws,
Respect is earned through fearsome claws.

Beneath the canopy of green,
A visage rarely ever seen.
King of shadows, night's disguise,
The ruler with the piercing eyes.

With every step, the forest bows,
To his highness, none oppose.
His empire vast, a vast expanse,
A dance of life, a timeless trance.

Within the depths where mysteries lie,
A silent watcher, passing by.
Highness of claws, so fierce, so grand,
Forever ruling, this untamed land.

Safari Sovereignty

Upon the golden grasp of dawn,
A realm where mighty beasts are drawn.
A king who all the creatures seek,
With power vast, and courage sleek.

In meadows wide, where zephyrs play,
The lion stands, surveys his sway.
His mane a banner in the breeze,
He rules beneath the ancient trees.

No army needs he, none but strength,
His kingdom runs for endless length.
A sovereign of an ageless land,
With regal paws, upon the sand.

Through savannahs, proud and bold,
He stands a ruler from days of old.
A sentinel of wild domains,
With grace and might, he ever reigns.

On safari trails, dreams take flight,
As he guards through day and night.
Sovereignty in every stride,
The lion rules with timeless pride.

Regal Roar

Beneath the skies where eagles soar,
Resounds a deep and regal roar.
A call that shakes the very ground,
In wild terrains, a king is crowned.

In dawn's first light and twilight's glow,
The echoes of his power flow.
A mantle pure of royal hue,
The lion roars, the world anew.

With each resounding mighty cry,
He speaks to earth and empty sky.
A testament of strength and grace,
A ruler none dare to replace.

Through valleys vast and hills afar,
His voice, a guiding primal star.
With every roar, his story told,
In lands of dust and tales of old.

In every breath a world ignites,
As day turns into starry nights.
Respected near, revered afar,
His regal roar, his mark, his scar.

Ruler's Rights

A scepter gleams in royal hand,
Commanding lands both far and wide,
With pow'rful voice that takes a stand,
To steer the ship through tempest tide.

In velvet robes adorned with grace,
A crown that weighs heavy with fate,
Beneath the gaze of time and space,
The ruler's rights do not abate.

From mountains high to valleys low,
Their word is law, their will is just,
Yet wisdom in each act must show,
Or kingdom's trust will turn to dust.

A leader's strength, a guiding light,
Through darkest nights and brightest days,
Throne's burden met with insight,
To carve the path in myriad ways.

Majesty's Measure

The measure of a majesty,
Is found in deeds, not words, alone,
In quiet acts of charity,
And justice met where wrongs are shown.

With every gesture, grand or small,
A legacy of light is laid,
Beneath the gilded, towering hall,
Where hopes of many are displayed.

The measure calls for wisdom's seed,
In choices made and battles fought,
For hearts to heal and minds to lead,
A ruler's worth by trials caught.

The golden scales of time reveal,
A majesty's true, lasting mark,
In shadows deep their truths conceal,
But in the light, they leave a spark.

Enchanter's Endowment

In twilight's realm where shadows play,
An enchanter's whispers weave the night,
With mystic words that softly sway,
Summoning dreams within their sight.

The gifted hand, by stars endowed,
Crafts illusions, bright and grand,
Among the cosmic dust and cloud,
The magic spreads through every land.

In ancient tomes, their secrets lie,
Guarded well by timeless spell,
A legacy that cannot die,
In stories old, where wonders swell.

Their power flows like river's course,
Through valleys deep and mountains high,
Changing hearts by gentle force,
Beneath the vast and endless sky.

Noble Excess

In halls of marble, rich and grand,
Where gold and velvet paint the scene,
The nobles' world is finely planned,
A tapestry of wealth, serene.

Yet in the midst of sparkling spoils,
Lies emptiness they can't disguise,
Amidst the laughter, gleaming oils,
Beneath the mask, a truth belies.

The finest wines, the rarest feast,
Cannot a weary soul sustain,
For noble hearts seek peace at least,
Beyond the glitz, beyond the gain.

The excess blinds, the riches bind,
True treasures in simplicity,
For in the gilded halls, we find,
The price of noble ecstasy.

Prowl of Royalty

In twilight's tender hush,
The lion makes his way,
Through grasslands rich and lush,
He claims the fading day.

Eyes like burning embers,
Survey the evening's spread,
Each movement he remembers,
This kingdom 'neath his tread.

A coat of golden splendor,
Reflects the dying light,
In silence soft and tender,
He merges with the night.

Majestic in his roaming,
His heart a warrior's drum,
While stars above are forming,
He knows his time has come.

Pride and power in motion,
This king without a throne,
Commands the world's devotion,
Yet walks his path alone.

Savanna's Legend

Beneath the sun's harsh glare,
The legend takes its turn,
In winds that tousle hair,
Old stories fiercely burn.

Across the endless plains,
This tale of strength and might,
Where courage never wanes,
And day dissolves to night.

Whispers in the grasses,
Of hunts from days of yore,
And every soul that passes,
Learns what came before.

Between each tick of silence,
The legend's heart beats true,
Through battles, storms, and violence,
Its essence will renew.

In shadows deep and narrow,
Lost dreams are intertwined,
For each sun's fallow marrow,
New heroes will we find.

Crowned Prowler

In midnight's velvet shroud,
The prowler finds his grace,
With steps both fierce and proud,
He claims his secret space.

Each moon shard marks his trail,
A crown above his brow,
Through silence he'll prevail,
No need to wonder how.

Beneath the canopy,
Where whispers dare to cease,
He moves with majesty,
In search of savage peace.

His eyes pierce through the black,
As night yields to his gaze,
In shadows he'll attack,
And dawn will sing his praise.

Regal in dark attire,
He roams without a sound,
A creature of desire,
In twilight's veil he's found.

Imperial of the Grasslands

With poise the lion strides,
Across the golden field,
In confidence he hides,
A strength that will not yield.

Regal, bold, and daunting,
He surveys his domain,
No threats seem all that haunting,
Beneath his royal reign.

The sun bestows its light,
Upon his tawny mane,
A symbol of his might,
In this vast, endless plain.

Each step is marked by grace,
A ruler of his kind,
An emblem of the chase,
With wisdom intertwined.

The grasslands bow and bend,
To welcome their great king,
In him, their hopes ascend,
Their songs of courage sing.

Sovereign Slice

A piece of night, the stars align,
In cosmic dance, they brightly shine,
A sovereign slice of time and space,
Eternal beauty, endless grace.

The moonlight weaves a silver thread,
Across the sky, where dreams are bred,
A tapestry of hopes and fears,
Woven through the celestial years.

Comets blaze a trail of light,
In heaven's realm, they take their flight,
A journey through the great unknown,
In solitude, they roam alone.

Each planet turns in silent grace,
A dance of orbs in boundless space,
The sovereign slice of life and death,
In cosmic symphony, they take breath.

O sovereign slice, where time is brief,
A fleeting moment's sweet relief,
In you, we find a sense of place,
A fragment of the vast embrace.

Apex Allocation

In the great expanse, the summit calls,
Where the eagle soars and starlight falls,
An apex of life's grand design,
Majestic peaks, so pure, divine.

To reach the top, we strive and strain,
Through trials, tears, and endless pain,
Yet there's a joy in each ascent,
A journey worth the effort spent.

The winds of fate, they lift us high,
Above the earth, towards the sky,
Through storms we pass, and through the calm,
We seek the apex with open palm.

Each step a testament to will,
A climb uphill, a mind to still,
In apex allocation found,
A peace within, a soul unbound.

On craggy heights, where eagles dine,
We touch the infinite, divine,
At apex, dreams and hopes combine,
To write our tale in heaven's sign.

Majestic Throne

Upon the mountain's highest crest,
There sits a throne, the most majestic,
A seat where kings of old would rest,
Within the clouds, high and mystic.

Beneath the dome of star-lit skies,
Where eagle's flight in silence swoops,
The throne awaits with open eyes,
Its ancient secrets tightly loops.

Rivers run in veins of earth,
Life's nectar flow from ancient stone,
In this realm of grandiose worth,
Resides the throne, eternal, lone.

The thunder's roar, the lightning's flash,
A symphony of nature's might,
In shadowed vale and craggy pass,
The throne endures the darkest night.

Majestic throne of time's embrace,
A beacon through the endless years,
In your fortress, we find our place,
Beyond our sorrows, hopes, and fears.

Jungle's Crown

Deep within the verdant green,
Where sunlight filters through the leaves,
A crown awaits, by few unseen,
In jungle's heart, where spirit breathes.

The rivers twist in serpentine,
Through ancient groves of towering trees,
A throne where wild things intertwine,
And nature whispers in the breeze.

Beneath the canopy so vast,
The echoes of a primal sound,
Tell tales of futures and of past,
In jungle's realm where life is crowned.

Creatures roam through shadowed glades,
In patterns old as earth and sky,
They guard the crown within the shades,
Where man and beast eye to eye.

O jungle's crown, your secrets deep,
In every fern and mossy mound,
Through you, our roots and bonds we keep,
In life's great circle, we are bound.

Noble Prowler

In the twilight's tender arms,
A shadow moves with grace,
Through the whispering boughs,
A noble prowler's trace.

Paws that silence fallen leaves,
Eyes like midnight's gleam,
Hunting through the velvet night,
A reverie unseen.

Strength within each measured step,
Silent, soft despair,
The world beneath those padded feet,
Knows not that he is there.

Guardians of the gleaming stars,
Guide him true and fair,
For in his heart, a fire burns,
A longing, laying bare.

The noble prowler roams tonight,
An echo of the past,
A spirit free, forever bound,
To shadows, deep and vast.

Dominance in Dawn

The sun ascends with amber light,
As shadows start to fade,
Dominance in dawn's embrace,
A regal beast, unafraid.

Mountains kiss the morning sky,
Rays caress their crest,
The sovereign of the waking world,
Stands vigilant, no rest.

His mane ablaze with dawning fire,
His roar the morning hymn,
The valleys tremble at the sound,
A reign both bold and grim.

In his eyes, the fate of all,
Predator and prey,
A kingdom ruled by primal law,
Where darkness yields to day.

Dominance in dawn's first light,
Proclaims a tale of power,
Nature's balance, fierce and true,
Awakening this hour.

Stalking Majesty

In the stillness of the night,
Beneath the moon's cold glance,
A figure moves with silent grace,
In an ancient, primal dance.

Eyes that pierce the silent dark,
Claws that skim the earth,
Each heartbeat stirs the forest's breath,
In measured, royal mirth.

Shadow's sleek and silent king,
A ghost among the trees,
With each soft step, a symphony,
To nature's quiet pleas.

Ebon fur in silver sheen,
The hunter takes his course,
Majestic in his endless stride,
An elemental force.

Stalking majesty at dusk,
Through wilderness he treads,
A sovereign of the untamed world,
Where wildest dreams are fed.

Vanquisher's Voice

In the heart of wilderness,
A sound begins to rise,
The vanquisher's voice resounds,
Beneath the open skies.

Echoes through the towering peaks,
And whispers through the glen,
A clarion call that chills the blood,
And silence breaks again.

With every note, the forest stills,
The rivers hush their flow,
For in that cry, the truth is told,
Of tales all creatures know.

Dominion claimed with fierce resolve,
No challenge left to fend,
The vanquisher's voice, a testament,
To battles, never end.

In twilight's fading, final hush,
His presence holds its sway,
For even in the darkest night,
His voice shall light the way.

Leader's Largesse

In halls of whisper, wise and grand,
A leader's heart, an open hand,
With vision clear, they chart the course,
A guiding light, a boundless force.

Their words inspire, ignite the flame,
With every deed, they carve their name,
A legacy of strength and grace,
In every heart, they find their place.

In darkest times, they stand tall,
Their courage answers every call,
Through storm and calm, they lead the way,
Turning night into bright day.

The smallest act, a grand intent,
In service, every moment spent,
With largesse, they shape the land,
A future built by gentle hand.

Their gift extends beyond the now,
With wisdom's touch, and firmest vow,
A legacy that time withstands,
Crafted by the leader's hands.

Alpha's Advantage

In forests deep, where shadows dance,
An alpha moves with measured glance,
With strength and skill, and eyes so bright,
They claim the night, they rule the night.

With every step, they mark the trail,
In presence strong, they shall prevail,
A guiding star for all to see,
In unity, they set minds free.

Their voice, a roar, commands respect,
Through every challenge, they deflect,
An alpha's heart, pure and strong,
Ensuring right from every wrong.

The pack is safe within their care,
No task too great, no burden spare,
Through thick and thin, their bond holds fast,
A future bold, from distant past.

And when the dawn begins to break,
Their legacy, no storm can shake,
In tales of old, their name will rise,
An alpha's strength, eternal prize.

Highness's Hand

Upon the throne, with grace and might,
A highness leads with vision bright,
With every word, and every deed,
They plant the seed, they meet the need.

A realm in balance, calm and fair,
The people's trust, their highest care,
With wisdom shared, and justice clear,
They quell the storm, they soothe the fear.

Their hand extends to rich and poor,
In each, they see a heart to restore,
Through peace and war, their will sustains,
A legacy where justice reigns.

To farthest land, their name does reach,
In every heart, their lessons teach,
With every act, they mold the day,
A world in light, in truth's array.

And when the time does call their rest,
Their reign remembered as the best,
In stories told, forever stand,
The grace and strength of highness's hand.

Majestic Marvel

In nature's grand and wondrous tale,
A marvel walks the timeless trail,
With every step, a story found,
In silence deep, profound, unbound.

The mountains sing their ancient song,
The rivers flow, both swift and long,
In every leaf, and sky so wide,
The marvel's voice, our hearts abide.

Majestic trees, they touch the sky,
In forests deep, where secrets lie,
With every creature, big and small,
The marvel cherishes them all.

The stars align, the heavens bright,
In every dawn, a new delight,
With every glance, and tender care,
They show the truth that love is share.

Through ages past, and future's time,
Their legacy, a song, a rhyme,
In every beat, the world will know,
Majestic marvel's endless glow.

Primacy's Prize

In the light of dawn, first rays break,
A world anew, beginning to wake.
Echoes of dreams, whispers of the wise,
This is the hour of primacy's prize.

Mountains stand tall, shadows recede,
Nature's bounty, a promise to heed.
A symphony of life, a timeless reprise,
Heralding the day with primacy's prize.

Rivers run wild, paths undefined,
Journeys unfold, fate intertwined.
In the heartbeat of time, where truth lies,
We uncover the gem, primacy's prize.

Skies painted gold, horizons expand,
Mysteries unravel, moments at hand.
In each breath taken, no room for disguise,
We grasp the essence of primacy's prize.

Stars will return, night will descend,
But this light, this dawn, on us it depends.
A legacy in the making, as time flies,
Forever we'll cherish primacy's prize.

Lionhearted Legacy

Beneath the banners of courage unfurled,
Bravery shines in an uncertain world.
Stories whispered through the ages prolonged,
Embers ignite where the lionhearted belonged.

With each step taken, battles they fought,
A spirit unbroken, a vision they sought.
In the annals of time, where memories thronged,
Lives the enduring lionhearted legacy, strong.

Roars of valor, echoes of the brave,
In the heart of turmoil, it's the legacy they gave.
Standing firm, where shadows have long,
Resides the power of the lionhearted's song.

Through trials and triumphs, every ordeal,
A testament of strength more than steel.
In every heart where courage is strong,
Echoes the eternal lionhearted's song.

Generations will follow, tales they will weave,
Of leaders who taught us to dare and to believe.
In the flow of time, through ages that belong,
Survives the immutable lionhearted legacy, long.

Apex Allotment

At the pinnacle where earth meets sky,
Ambitions soar, dreams can defy.
In the realm of the chosen, where few arise,
Lies the reward, the apex allotment's prize.

Steps forged in perseverance, trials overcome,
Paths undefined, routing ambitions' drum.
In moments where clarity floods the eyes,
One ascends to the apex allotment's skies.

Mountaintops whisper secrets kept,
Awakening spirits where success is met.
In the silence where aspirations rise,
Awaits the embrace of the apex allotment's ties.

Journeys culminate, and visions complete,
In the end, fulfillment tastes so sweet.
Up on high, where destiny lies,
Resides the gift of the apex allotment's sighs.

Though descents ensue, and valleys call,
In the heart, that peak stands tall.
Always remembered, through lows and highs,
Remains the triumph, the apex allotment's prize.

Majesty's Merit

In courts adorned with regal grace,
The light of wisdom casts its lace.
From throne to heart, history's spirit,
Speaks the truth of majesty's merit.

Crowns and sceptres, symbols of reign,
Each echoes a ruler's joy and pain.
Through actions bold, with honor's credit,
We learn the breadth of majesty's merit.

From fields of battle to halls serene,
The virtues of leadership are seen.
In each act of kindness, in justice explicit,
Resides the core of majesty's merit.

Against the tide of betrayal's tide,
With nobility's fire, rulers stride.
In the chronicles written, deeds are knit,
Unfolding the story of majesty's merit.

As ages pass, rulers may fall,
But the essence of merit stands tall.
In every heart, where truth shall sit,
Lives the legacy of majesty's merit.

Apex Ruler

In the forest, whispers spread,
Tales of the one all creatures dread.
Eyes of fire, stance refined,
Commanding all with mind aligned.

Paws that tread as soft as silk,
In shadows, like the calmest ilk.
Beneath the moon, his roar is law,
In his kingdom, none have flaw.

Majestic as the tallest pine,
Strength and grace in pure design.
He prowls his realm, the night obeys,
And every heart in silence sways.

Apex Ruler, sovereign might,
Guided by the unseen light.
In the hunt, his fierce decree,
Nature bows to his decree.

Time itself bears witness true,
To the legacy that scents ensue.
King eternal, forest bound,
Revered in silence, night exhaled sound.

Guardian of Herds

In the vast and golden plain,
Where freedom's beams do compassionate reign,
A sentinel stands with eyes so wise,
Guarding life 'neath endless skies.

Horns that spiral, mark of grace,
Stalwart spirit, calm of face.
Beneath them gather, young and old,
Safe from shadows, strong and bold.

Through the dawn and twilight veil,
He endures each storm and trail.
A gentle leader, humble, grand,
Defends their sanctuary of land.

Upon the winds his watchful eye,
Counts each star and moon in sky.
Protector of the roaming souls,
In his vigilance, the world feels whole.

Guardian of Herds, revered might,
In plains so vast, day to night.
Softly humming life's refrain,
Ensures the herds will roam again.

Clawed Monarch

In caverns deep where shadows dance,
Resides a ruler, fierce perchance.
With talons sharp and gaze that burns,
Balance of strength the world discerns.

Wings that span the breadth of dreams,
Tales of power in golden gleams.
A heart that beats with ancient lore,
Echoes of thunder, wildly roar.

An empire vast, from ridge to ridge,
He guards with might the ancient bridge.
Wisdom borne of endless nights,
Guides his flight through starlit heights.

Upon the crags and cliffs he reigns,
A guardian of the stormy plains.
In every beat and every claw,
Nature's rhythm, archaic law.

Clawed Monarch, fierce, serene,
In realms where dusk and dawn convene.
A king in feathers, scales and fire,
By night he soars, our hearts aspire.

Grassland Guardian

Where the horizons blend and meet,
The grass waves warm in endless beat.
A figure stands, alert and still,
Protector of the rolling hill.

Fur aglow in sunlit hue,
Sleek and nimble, always true.
Eyes that trace the wind's embrace,
Echo whispers, secrets to chase.

Through the seasons, cold and warm,
He braves the heart of every storm.
A silent sentinel of hope,
In twilight's fall, he learns to cope.

Each morning's cry, each silent night,
He guards the land from dawn's first light.
In his watch, the wild remains,
Untouched, untamed, the endless plains.

Grassland Guardian, steadfast, bright,
Harnesses day and shields the night.
In fields that stretch where dreams have trod,
He holds the line, as if by God.

Dominion's Portion

In the realm where shadows dance,
Emotions flare in silent trance,
Dominion claims its fateful chance,
In the court of circumstance.

Stars above, a watchful blaze,
Light the night with ancient gaze,
Upon the world, the kingdom lays,
Dreams unfold in myriad ways.

Winds whisper through the emerald trees,
Carrying tales across the seas,
A sovereign's heart in endless pleas,
Bound by time's ephemeral breeze.

Through the valleys, over peaks,
Echoed voices, wisdom speaks,
History in whispers seeks,
Life's journey, tender streaks.

Beneath the moon's benevolent light,
Kingdoms rise and fade from sight,
In the quiet of the night,
Dominion claims its soaring flight.

Pride's Dominion

On the plains where lions roam,
Each step they take, they claim their home,
In the heart, the pride has grown,
From lush grass to steely loam.

Where the sun meets the ground,
Echoes of the mighty sound,
Strength in numbers, tightly bound,
Through the wilds, so profound.

In the eyes of beasts so bold,
Stories of the ages told,
Silent glories they behold,
Legends etched in fields of gold.

Beneath the stars' celestial map,
Around the watering hole's trap,
Generations blaze a lap,
Nature's endless, timeless wrap.

In the pulse where nature's rife,
Balance found in dawn and strife,
Pride's dominion springs to life,
A testament to primal life.

Sovereign's Share

Underneath the azure sky,
Where the wild winds pass by,
Sovereign's share none can deny,
Anchored deep, yet dreams can fly.

Summits high and valleys wide,
Nature's secrets they can't hide,
Every stream and every tide,
Whispers tales from far and wide.

Through the forest, shadows play,
In the kingdom of the fey,
Mystic realms where night meets day,
Ancient spirits find their sway.

Meadows green with morning dew,
Hues embracing every view,
Hear the call, the sovereign's cue,
In the heart, the land renew.

From dawn till dusk, the sovereign's grace,
Paints the earth in warm embrace,
Every step in time and space,
Claiming all in its vast chase.

Monarch's Bounty

Golden hues at break of dawn,
Fields of plenty, freshly drawn,
Monarch's bounty, nature's pawn,
Life anew, from night till morn.

Harvest rich and rivers gleam,
In the monarch's grandest dream,
Every whisper, every beam,
Sculpting life and every theme.

In the silence of twilight,
Stars above in quiet flight,
Bounty's yield, the monarch's right,
Echoes loud through endless night.

Wanderers with hearts so pure,
Find the paths that they're unsure,
In the bounty, they secure,
Monarch's grace, forevermore.

Earth and sky in perfect blend,
A timeless tale they both defend,
Bounty vast with no end,
Monarch's blessings ever send.

Top Claim

On peaks where eagles dare to glide,
A claim to heights we can't deny.
In whispers soft the mountains sigh,
The top, where endless dreams abide.

In rugged paths, our strength is tried,
With every step, the soul takes flight.
The night prepares to banish night,
On this ascent, we'll not be tied.

With courage born from winds so wide,
We climb where stars adorn the sky.
Seeking truths we can't belie,
Our spirits bound, yet undenied.

Each moment spent, each breath applied,
Draws closer to the summit high.
In nature's lap, we unify,
Our hearts in triumph, magnified.

So onward, with our hearts allied,
We chase the dreams that never die.
In every stone, the stories lie,
Of those who rose where limits tried.

Rule Redeemed

In shadows cast by past regime,
A light begins to softly gleam.
From ruins dark, we birth a dream,
A rule redeemed, a new esteem.

Where tyrants trod with hearts of steam,
We find a path, a purest beam.
Through unity, the chosen theme,
We rise above the foul extreme.

With every voice, a crystal scream,
For justice fair, the sacred scheme.
Our spirits dream, our faces beam,
In harmony, we form a team.

No longer bound by cruel regime,
We chart a course through hope's esteem.
In every heart, a hopeful theme,
A rule redeemed, a golden dream.

So let us shine, a mighty stream,
Of light and love, a shared extreme.
In every life, a radiant gleam,
Where once was dark, now reigns supreme.

Sovereign's Selection

In courts where whispers weave their tales,
A sovereign's choice, the heart prevails.
With wisdom, grace, the spirit sails,
On destiny's vast, shifting gales.

In eyes that see beyond the veils,
The truth in shadows, never pales.
Through trials harsh and whispered trails,
A leader's course, the heart unveils.

With scepter drawn, a path details,
Of justice pure, where love assails.
Through every storm, a voice regales,
The sovereign's choice, where peace entails.

Through ancient laws and modern scales,
The balance kept, no justice fails.
A harmony that life entails,
In sovereign's hand, each heart exalts.

So let the anthem's purest tales,
Proclaim the choice that never pales.
In every heart, this truth impales,
The sovereign's choice, forever hails.

In the Lion's Grasp

In jungles deep where shadows clasp,
The lion holds its mighty grasp.
With roars that echo, hearts to rasp,
A dance of life, no soul to lapse.

In amber eyes where secrets rasp,
The wild unfurls its ancient asp.
With strength and grace that none can clasp,
The lion reigns, no fear to grasp.

Through nights of stars and moonlight's gasp,
The hunt begins with silent rasp.
In every step, a power's clasp,
Within the heart, the wild's grasp.

In dawn's first light, the moments clasp,
A kingdom ruled by nature's rasp.
From birth to dusk, life's endless gasp,
In lion's heart, the wild's grasp.

So let us heed the jungle's grasp,
Where life and death together clasp.
In lion's world, a sacred rasp,
The wild remains, its truths to grasp.

Sovereignty in Stripes

Beneath the sun's relentless glare,
The orange stripes do flare,
In shadow, they stealthily move,
An air of mystique they prove.

Rivers whisper secrets bold,
Tales of tigers, fierce and old,
Their kingdom stretched from hill to shore,
In their pride, they forever soar.

With a growl, their might displayed,
In the jungle, power weighed,
Paws that tread on ancient ground,
In their domain, they wear the crown.

Echoes of a past so vast,
Legends in the shadow cast,
Golden eyes that pierce the night,
In sovereignty, they claim their right.

Monarchs of the forest green,
In their presence, nature's queen,
Stripes that mark their regal call,
In their reign, they appal.

Rule of the Roarer

Upon the plains, the lion strides,
Among the grasses, where life hides,
With each step, the ground does quake,
In his eyes, the dawn does break.

His mane, aflame with golden light,
In the day and darkest night,
Ears attuned to silent plea,
His is the law of land and sea.

From the hills to the distant shore,
All respect the lion's roar,
In his gaze, the wild is still,
In his presence, bend to will.

The herd moves to ancient call,
Knowing well he'll stand or fall,
Beneath the acacias stretching far,
His reign is marked by each scar.

In twilight's hush, he walks alone,
His kingdom's every rock and stone,
Majesty in every stride,
In his rule, the steadfast guide.

Mighty Roar

In the heart of jungle deep,
Where shadows in silence creep,
A mighty roar splits the air,
Proclaiming dominion there.

Teeth like ivory, sharp and bright,
Eyes that conquer darkest night,
With a leap and a fearless stride,
The jungle's king cannot hide.

All creatures tremble, great and small,
As the echo of his call,
Resounds through dense and tangled trees,
Carried by the whispered breeze.

From dawn to dusk, his power reigns,
On rugged paths and endless plains,
A symphony of dominance,
In every growl, every glance.

Majesty in flesh and bone,
His presence, ancient stone,
For in his roar, the earth does sing,
An ode to nature's fiercest king.

Savannah's Strength

Golden waves in endless dance,
Under sun's relentless glance,
The heartbeat of the endless plain,
Where giants roam, an untamed reign.

With tusks that speak of battles won,
And scars that glint in setting sun,
Elephants tread with steady grace,
Their strength etched on the earth's face.

Lions lounge in shadows cast,
Guardians of stories past,
Their might is felt in every breeze,
A power that puts all at ease.

Giraffes stretch to reach the sky,
Leaves that drift and float on by,
In their stillness, calm resides,
Strength in peace, where life abides.

From zebra's stripe to cheetah's speed,
Each plays a part, each fills a need,
In savannah's vast and wild embrace,
Strength and grace in every place.

Ruling Claws

In shadows vast, the jungle speaks,
Of prowling kings with silent strides.
Their amber eyes in moonlit peaks,
Through verdant realms, the night abides.

With every leap, the forest stirs,
A ghostly hush, a whisper heard.
The monarchs rule where darkness blurs,
Claws of power, untamed word.

Beneath the canopy's green veil,
A kingdom fierce and wild prevails.
With roaring might, their tales regale,
Ruling claws, and unbeaten trails.

In dawn's first light, secrets shroud,
Where creatures bow, both meek and proud.
Nature's laws in silence loud,
By these sovereign beasts are vowed.

Amber eyes and fangs of night,
Guardians of the primal right.
In their reign, no sound, no sight,
Fades the power of ruling might.

Fierce Inferno

Flames leap high, a crimson dance,
In twilight's whispered, fevered trance.
Embers glow with fierce romance,
Casting sparks in wild advance.

Winds of wrath feed raging flames,
They spiral high, no one tames.
Nature's fury, no one blames,
In this fierce inferno's games.

From the ashes, phoenix rise,
Rebirth in fire, a grand surprise.
In the blaze, new life lies,
Strength and valor in their eyes.

Beneath the stars, the fire roars,
A passion deep within it pours.
Tales of old, legends' lore,
Of fierce infernos at its core.

Heat so fierce, it scars the night,
A beacon in the dark, so bright.
In its heart, a guiding light,
Fierce inferno's endless flight.

Plains' Majesty

Wide expanse of golden green,
Whispers soft in fields serene.
Beneath the sky, so vast, so keen,
Majesty of plains unseen.

Horizon's edge, where heavens meet,
Stretch of land beneath my feet.
An endless sea in rhythmic beat,
Plains' wonders pure and sweet.

With every breeze, the grasses sway,
Nature's dance in wild array.
In sunlit hues, the colors play,
Majesty of plains at bay.

Where shadows drift and creatures roam,
This boundless land forever home.
In silence loud, and vast unknown,
Plains' majesty has grown.

Under skies of azure blue,
In every dawn, a world anew.
Plains so grand, and ever true,
Majestic scenes, in soul imbue.

Sovereignty Under Sun

Beneath the gilded, blazing orb,
A realm where every beam absorbed.
In sunlit courts, the skies adorn,
Sovereignty at every dawn.

Mountains high and valleys deep,
Under sun's golden sweep.
Sovereign lands where shadows sleep,
In warmth, the earth, its secrets keep.

By day's embrace, in gilded hue,
A kingdom spreads in every view.
With royal light, the sky imbues,
Sovereignty the sun renews.

In every ray, the power gleams,
A reign of light in waking dreams.
Sovereignty flows in brilliant streams,
Nature's rule where sunlight beams.

Under the sun, the world unfurls,
A sovereign throne in radiant pearls.
In light's embrace, life twirls,
Sovereignty, the day impels.

Courage of the Mane

In shadows deep, the lion waits
Emboldened heart, defying fate
With every step, the earth does quake
A fearless roar, no chain can break

Sunrise gilds his golden form
He braves the night, he rides the storm
A beacon 'midst the growing dark
In silent strength, he leaves his mark

Through fields of strife, his spirit soars
To distant calls, his courage roars
Unyielding gaze, so fierce, so bright
A guardian in the dead of night

In twilight's haze, the legend grows
A tale of might the jungle knows
With bated breath, the world will see
The lion's dance with destiny

Underneath the starlit canopy
In realms where shadows cease to be
He paves the way, both bold and free
An emblem of tenacity

Pride's Regent

On verdant plains where echoes ring
The lion strides, the jungle king
His kingdom vast, his reign is true
Beneath the skies, in wide review

With piercing eyes, he scans the land
His loyal pride at his command
In loyalty, their fate entwined
A royal bond, forever bind

Through ancient paths and trails unseen
He rules with poise, both fierce and keen
With every roar, he claims the night
A sovereign force, a regal might

Along the river, through the grass
His silent steps, they lightly pass
In hunting grounds where shadows meet
He finds his throne with steady feat

Beneath the ancient baobab's shade
His lineage rests, a legacy made
From dawn to dusk, his tale profound
In whispers of the wild, resound

Crown of the Serengeti

In realms where golden pastures spread
Where twilight skies in blush are laid
The lion walks, a crown unseen
In tapestry of gold and green

His mane, a halo in the dusk
Amidst the grass, so tall, so husk
With measured stride, through lands untamed
The Serengeti's pride proclaimed

At dusk, he claims the setting sun
With whispered secrets, journeys won
His regal stance, a timeless flow
In valleys wide, where rivers go

Moonlight dances on his domain
With shadows long, in vast refrain
A symphony of night and light
He reigns supreme, in endless flight

Through winds that sing of ancient lore
He treads with grace upon the floor
The whispering world beneath his paws
In silent reverie, he draws

Emperor of Sunlit Grass

In fields where sunlight kisses brown
The lion wears an unseen crown
His eyes, a glimpse of morning stars
Survey the land, where horizons are

In lengths of green, he finds his path
With every step, the world's caress
The emperor of sunlit grass
In regal air, his presence vast

Through silent woods, on velvet paws
He wanders through the emerald draws
With every breath, the earth he feels
A kingly grace within him steals

The day unfolds, his realm is bright
In fields of gold, in waves of light
Majestic mane, as banners fly
In sunlit sea, under open sky

In whispered winds, his story lives
Through tranquil plains, his spirit gives
A legacy of courage bred
Upon the earth where he is led

First Cut

In fields where morning's dew yet clings,
The scythe begins its sweeping sings,
A blade so pure, it meets the grain,
The first cut of a harvest's gain.

Gold stalks bow low with rustling breath,
As if they knew they faced their death,
Yet spring will bring their kind again,
In endless cycles, nature's plan.

The farmer's hands are rough and worn,
By countless dawns and frosty morn,
Each cut a promise, sworn and true,
To feed the many, brave the few.

And as the sun bids sky farewell,
The harvest's tale is left to tell,
From first cut to the bushel's brim,
Life's rhythm in a scythe's hymn.

So rest tonight, beneath the stars,
With dreams of grain and open bars,
For morning brings the labor's cheer,
In fields where first cuts persevere.

Royal Ration

Upon the throne of golden glaze,
Where kings and queens in splendor daze,
The royal ration, blissful taste,
In banquet grand, it lays to waste.

Gilded platters, feast's array,
A kingdom's finest on display,
From vineyards vast to orchards wide,
The earth's abundance, none to hide.

The clink of crystal, cheer in echoes,
A dance of flavors, rich as meadows,
Each bite a tale of distant lands,
Each sip a secret from the sands.

Attendants clad in silken grace,
With measured steps and stately pace,
Serve treasures rare on silv'ry trays,
Amidst the court's admiring gaze.

For though the night extends its fall,
With shadows cast on ancient wall,
The royal ration, feast's delight,
Will linger long past morning's light.

Lion's Claim

In the heart of the savannah's gold,
Where amber grasses sweetly fold,
The lion makes his steadfast claim,
A ruler fierce, untamed, untamed.

Beneath the sky of endless blue,
His kingdom vast, his pride in view,
With roars that echo through the plain,
He holds his court, his noble reign.

The zebra fleet and buffalo strong,
Move warily within his song,
For in his eyes they see the fire,
Of instincts old and swift desire.

The dusk brings shadows, cool relief,
Yet even then, in night's belief,
The lion's claim stands true and bold,
A legacy from days of old.

So walks he through the twilight's mist,
A sovereign no one dare resist,
With every step, his power flows,
The lion's claim, the wild bestows.

Majestic Margin

Where oceans kiss the rocky shore,
A boundary drawn forevermore,
The margin of the earth's embrace,
Majestic in its timeless grace.

The waves that carve the ancient stone,
Speak whispers of an age unknown,
With every crash and foamy leap,
They secrets of the deep seas keep.

High cliffs that stand against the tide,
In silent strength and towering pride,
Witness to the winds that wail,
And stories in the stormy gale.

Above the seagulls wheel and cry,
In the endless blue of sky,
Their flights a dance in freedom's name,
Above the margin's wild frame.

So let us wander to the edge,
And ponder life upon this ledge,
Majestic margin, vast and grand,
A meeting of both sea and land.

Dominion of the Pride

In the golden realm, the lion roars,
His voice a thunder, wild and free,
Underneath the endless azure skies,
He claims the land, his regal decree.

Through whispering grass and ancient trees,
His gaze surveys the rolling plains,
A kingdom vast, with secrets deep,
Where power, grace, and wisdom reign.

His mane ablaze with the dawn's first light,
Each stride a testament of might,
The shadows yield beneath his glance,
In this domain, the stars align.

With silent pads on sunlit trails,
His presence felt, yet seldom seen,
Eternal watch upon the veldt,
The pride's protector, fierce, serene.

When twilight paints the sky in hues,
The lion stands, a timeless guide,
Dominion holds, the pride remains,
Forever strong, side by side.

Ruler of the Veldt

Beneath the sunlit canopy,
The ruler strides in sovereign grace,
A whisper of the ages past,
Within his eyes, the ancient chase.

Echoes of the hunt resound,
Through valleys lush, and rivers wide,
His noble heart beats firm and sure,
Across the veldt, his spirit flies.

The velvet dusk of twilight falls,
An empire at the horizon's edge,
He stands alone upon his throne,
A promise kept, a silent pledge.

His mane a crown of golden strands,
Each breath a testament of power,
In every glance, a legacy,
The ruler reigns, the final hour.

In moonlit glades and fields of gold,
The stories whispered on the breeze,
Of ancient kings and battles won,
His legacy, the land's heart frees.

Realm of Claws

Within the realm of claws and might,
The savanna breathes a primal song,
Where hunters prowl and shadows blend,
The call of wild, both fierce and long.

Paws that tread on sacred ground,
Echoes in the nocturnal air,
With every strike, the balance kept,
In claws' embrace, the wildness fair.

Through ancient paths and hidden trails,
The cycle spins, eternal turn,
In this domain of tooth and claw,
The fires of life and death still burn.

A dance of strength and subtle grace,
Played out beneath the cosmic dome,
In realms of claws, where spirits soar,
Each heartbeat brings them further home.

The twilight whispers secrets deep,
Of battles fought and victories won,
In claws' embrace, the world survives,
Under the watch of the eternal sun.

Savanna's Monarch

Upon the plains where shadows play,
The monarch walks with measured stride,
His kingdom vast beneath the skies,
Where endless fields and rivers bide.

A gaze that pierces through the veil,
Of dusk and dawn, both fierce and grand,
In every roar, a legacy,
A tale of power carved in sand.

The savanna hums its ancient tune,
A symphony of life and death,
The monarch strides through grasslands wide,
With every step, a world rebirth.

In regal poise, he claims the night,
A sentinel of stars and moon,
His realm a testament of strength,
Beneath the sky's celestial rune.

The wind that sweeps the open land,
Carries his legend far and near,
For savanna's heart, he is the pulse,
The monarch's reign both strong and clear.

Wild Monarch

In fields where flowers sway and bend,
A monarch flutters, wings extend.
Golden hues that catch the light,
A graceful dance in morning's sight.

From milkweed stems its life does start,
A caterpillar sets apart.
Transformed it takes a wondrous flight,
The wild monarch, pure delight.

Through breeze and warmth it makes its way,
In search of blooms and skies of gray.
A fleeting beauty, summer's child,
The wild monarch, free and wild.

Upon the wind its journey pressed,
In nature's arms it finds its rest.
A legacy in amber sealed,
Monarch of the wild field.

The seasons shift, the chill does come,
Yet whispers of its flight still hum.
A fleeting brush with nature's art,
The wild monarch, in each heart.

Desert Despot

Beneath the sun's relentless blaze,
The barren land, a dusty maze.
A figure stands with shadows long,
The desert despot, harsh and strong.

No fertile fields, no rivers near,
Just endless dunes where none appear.
With steely eyes and unbowed will,
The desert despot, standing still.

The wind doth howl, the sand does sting,
No gentleness this land doth bring.
A cruel command o'er harsh terrain,
The desert despot, ever reigns.

Oasis fleeting, mirage near,
A thirst unquenched, a distant tear.
Amidst the harsh, a rule so stark,
The desert despot, leaves its mark.

Beneath the night, the stars so bright,
A moment's peace from day's cruel bite.
Yet dawn returns with burning face,
The desert despot, holds its place.

Pride's Guardian

In shadows deep beneath the trees,
A sentinel among the leaves.
With watchful gaze and heart so true,
The pride's guardian, ever through.

A growl that rumbles through the night,
Protects the pride from fear and fright.
With strength unmatched and courage fierce,
The pride's guardian, none can pierce.

Through trials faced and dangers braved,
The path for kin, in blood it paved.
A noble heart, a steadfast mind,
The pride's guardian, left behind.

In twilight's glow, a figure grand,
Defends the realm with gentle hand.
A legacy of honor near,
The pride's guardian, ever dear.

At dawn anew, the watch is set,
Through bounding plains and sunset met.
In every heart, a beat remains,
The pride's guardian, through the veins.

Prowling King

In twilight's hush, a shadow forms,
A prowling king through forest storms.
He moves with grace through night's embrace,
A sovereign in this wild place.

His eyes aglow with ancient fire,
In him, the heartbeat of the dire.
The moonlight casts a silent ring,
Around the steps of the prowling king.

With every stride, the earth does bow,
Respect through time, both then and now.
A legacy of strength and might,
The prowling king, a fearsome sight.

Yet in his roar, there's more than power,
A story told at midnight hour.
Of wisdom gained through battles won,
The prowling king, revered by none.

He fades into the night once more,
A legend weaved in whispered lore.
Forever etched in nature's song,
The prowling king where he belongs.

Majestic Divide

Mountains touch the sky above,
Where eagles soar and winds do rove.
A boundary drawn in nature's hand,
A line where earth and sky expand.

Rivers carve their ancient course,
Whispering tales with gentle force.
Between the peaks, valleys wide,
Nature's grand and majestic divide.

Forests dense with secrets old,
Legends in their shadows told.
Time stands still where growth is wild,
In nature's book, each page compiled.

Snow-capped summits kiss the blue,
A sight to see, a breathtaking view.
In silence, whispers softly ride,
Across the vast, majestic divide.

Mists arise as day does break,
Nature's canvas, a dawn to wake.
Boundary drawn with lines so wide,
The harmony of a majestic divide.

Unequal Spoils

In markets where the coin is king,
Voices rise, yet sorrows sing.
Gold and silver stacked so high,
Look and see the rich man's sky.

But beneath the wealth and gain,
Lies a land of silent pain.
The spoils gathered, unevenly shared,
Leaving many in despair.

Riches flaunted, gleaming bright,
A stark contrast to the night.
Where hunger gnaws and dreams collapse,
In the unequal spoils gap.

Beneath the surface, shadows weave,
Stories of those who silently grieve.
For the spoils are not equally spread,
A tale of tears, where hope is dead.

When shall justice touch the ground,
Where unequal spoils abound?
A dream for all, to equally share,
In a world more just, and fair.

Kingdom's Claim

Castles rise from ancient stone,
In lands where valiant heroes roamed.
A kingdom's claim on earth so vast,
Echoes from a noble past.

Knights with banners, shining bright,
Guard the realm with all their might.
In fields where battles once did rage,
Legends write each passing age.

Crowned with honor, lands they tread,
Where history and myth are wed.
Banners flutter, tales proclaim,
In the heart of the kingdom's claim.

Rivers flow through fields of green,
Nature sings where glory's been.
A throne of earth, with skies untamed,
Mark the lines of a kingdom's claim.

Echoes whisper through the halls,
Of fortresses with shadowed walls.
In every stone, a hero's name,
Laid in the legacy of the kingdom's claim.

Regal Slice

In banquet halls where chandeliers gleam,
Nobles dine and dancers dream.
A slice of life so richly hued,
Where stories of the court are viewed.

Goblets raised in silent toast,
To the fortunes they do boast.
A regal slice of grandeur pure,
For the elite, it does endure.

Velvet curtains, whispers light,
Mark the secrets of the night.
In chambers grand where shadows lie,
Underneath a starry sky.

Among their riches, gems, and gold,
Tales of grandeur are retold.
A life of splendor, fine, precise,
In every moment, a regal slice.

Yet beyond the ivory gate,
Lives less grand await their fate.
While inside, they sing and dice,
To celebrate their regal slice.

Milton Keynes UK
Ingram Content Group UK Ltd.
UKHW020723090824
446757UK00010B/507